Unholy Sonnets

BOOKS BY MARK JARMAN

POETRY

UNHOLY SONNETS
Story Line Press, 2000

QUESTIONS FOR ECCLESIASTES
Story Line Press, 1997

IRIS
Story Line Press, 1992

THE BLACK RIVIERA
Wesleyan University Press, 1990

FAR AND AWAY
Carnegie-Mellon University Press, 1985

THE ROTE WALKER
Carnegie-Mellon University Press, 1981

NORTH SEA
Cleveland State University Poetry Center, 1978

ANTHOLOGY

REBEL ANGELS: 25 POETS OF THE NEW FORMALISM
Edited by Mark Jarman and David Mason
Story Line Press, 1996

CRITICISM

THE REAPER ESSAYS
by Mark Jarman and Robert McDowell
Story Line Press, 1996

Unholy Sonnets

POEMS BY

MARK JARMAN

STORY LINE PRESS

2000

Published by Story Line Press, Inc., Three Oaks Farm, P.O. Box 1240, Ashland, OR 97520-0055

This publication was made possible thanks in part to the generous support of the Nicholas Roerich Museum, the Andrew W. Mellon Foundation, the San Francisco Foundation and our individual contributors.

Cover design by Lysa McDowell
Painting, "Albion Rose" (Glad Day) by William Blake, reprinted courtesy of the Huntington Library, Art Collections, and Botanical Gardens, San Marino, California.

ACKNOWLEDGMENTS

Grateful acknowledgment is given to the following periodicals where some of these poems appeared, sometimes with different numbers or titles.

Atlanta Review: 33; *Bellingham Review:* 25; 31; *The Cortland Review:* 21; 24; 26; 32; *The Connecticut Review:* 1; *Crab Orchard Review:* 39; *The Denver Quarterly:* 13; 23; 42; *The Flannery O'Connor Bulletin:* 8; *The Formalist:* 29; 46; *The Gettysburg Review:* 5; 44; *The Hudson Review:* 2; 3; 12; 14; 18; 34; *Image:* 4; 15; 35; *Kenyon Review:* 9; 10; *New Letters:* 6; 22; *New Virginia Review:* 45; *Oxford American:* 11; *Prairie Schooner:* 28; 36; *Quarterly West:* 7; *Sewanee Review:* 19; 27; 43; *Shenandoah:* 17; 41; *Solo:* 40; *Epilogue; The Southern Review:* 16; *Southwest Review:* 30; *Tar River Poetry: Prologue;* 38; *Third Coast:* 20; 47; *Two Rivers Review:* 37; *The Yale Review:* 48

"The Word 'Answer'" (1) was included in *the Best American Poetry 1998.* "The World" (48) was included in *Contemporary American Poetry: A Bread Loaf Anthology.*

Heartfelt thanks to Andrew Hudgins, Dennis Sampson, and Terri Witek who read this book in earlier versions and offered valuable suggestions.

TABLE OF CONTENTS

For Amy

I shall be made thy Musique

John Donne

Wert thou my enemy, O thou my friend

Gerard Manley Hopkins

Please be the driver bearing down behind,
Or swerve in front and slow down to a crawl,
Or leave a space to lure me in, then pull
Ahead, cutting me off, and blast your horn.
Please climb the mountain with me, tailgating
And trying to overtake on straightaways.
Let nightfall make us both pick up the pace,
Trading positions with our high beams glaring.
And when we have exhausted sanity
And fuel, and smoked our engines, then, please stop,
Lurching onto the shoulder of the road,
And get out, raging, and walk up to me,
Giving me time to feel my stomach drop,
And see you face to face, and say, "My Lord!"

I

1 THE WORD "ANSWER"

"Prayer exerts an influence upon God's action, even
upon his existence. This is what the word 'answer' means."
Karl Barth, Prayer

Lightning walks across the shallow seas,
Stick figures putting feet down hard
Among the molecules. Meteors dissolve
And drop their pieces in a mist of iron,
Drunk through atomic skin like dreamy wine.
The virus that would turn a leaf dark red
Seizes two others that would keep it green.
They spread four fingers like a lizard's hand.
Into this random rightness comes the prayer,
A change of weather, a small shift of degree
That heaves a desert where a forest sweated,
And asks creation to return an answer.
That's all it wants: a prayer just wants an answer,
And twists time in a knot until it gets it.

There's the door. Will anybody get it?
That's what he's wondering; the bath's still warm;
And by the time he towels off and puts on
His pajamas, robe, and slippers and goes down,
They'll be gone, won't they? There's the door again;
And nobody's here to answer it but him.
Perhaps they'll go away. But it's not easy,
Relaxing in the tub, reading the paper,
With someone at the front door, ringing and pounding,

And—that sounds like glass—breaking in.
At least the bathroom door's securely bolted.
Or is that any assurance in this case?
He might as well go find out what's the matter.
Whoever it is must really want . . . something.

We ask for bread, he makes his body bread.
We ask for daily life, and every day,
We get a life, or a facsimile,
Or else we get a tight place in a crowd
Or test results with the prognosis—bad.
We ask and what is given is the answer,
For we can always see it as an answer,
Distorted as it may be, from our God.
What shall we ask for then? For his return,
Like the bereaved parents with the monkey's paw,
Wishing, then wishing again? The last answer,
When we have asked for all that we can ask for,
May be the end of time, our mangled child,
And in the doorway, dead, the risen past.

With this prayer I am making up a God
On a gray day, prophesying snow.
I pray that God be immanent as snow
When it has fallen thickly, a deep God.
With this prayer I am making up a God
Who answers prayer, responding like the snow
To footprints and the wind, to a child in snow
Making an angel who will speak for God.

God, I am thinking of you now as snow,
Descending like the answer to a prayer,
This prayer that you will be made visible,
Drifting and deepening, a dazzling, slow
Acknowledgment, out of the freezing air,
As dangerous as it is beautiful.

2

Which is the one, which of the imps inside
Unglues itself from the yin-yang embrace
Of its good twin or its bad twin and plays
The angel advocate, the devil's guide?
Which blob of conscience, like a germicide,
Catches and kills the impulse when it strays?
Which impulse with light playing on its face,
Its fright mask, leads to the dark outside?

All of them shapeless feelings given form
By words which they in turn give substance to.
As particle and wave make light, they swarm
Together with their names. And we do, too,
Praying that God knows each of us and cares
About the things we speak of in our prayers.

3

Soften the blow, imagined God, and give
Me one good reason for this punishment.
Where does the pressure come from? Is it meant
To kill me in the end or help me live?
My thoughts about you are derivative.
Still, I believe a part of me is bent
To make your grace look like an accident
And keep my soul from being operative.
But if I'm to be bent back like the pole
A horseshoe clangs against and gives a kink to,
Then take me like the grinning iron monger
I saw once twist a bar that made him sink to
His knees. His tongue was like a hot pink coal
As he laughed and said he thought that he was stronger.

4

I think of Gosse, watching his father paint
Anemones from tidal pools in Devon
(Long plundered by the time Gosse called them back).
All the boy knew of art were these water colors
With Latin names for captions, an extravagance
Indulged for science, checked by a firm faith.
And there was also the book his father wrote
To reconcile the Bible and Charles Darwin—
Greeted with scorn. I think of Gosse writing
About the days alone with his mother's illness
And afterwards with his father's loneliness.
He saw and heard the marine biologist pray
As if he could, by word and gesture only,
Pry open the mute heavens like a bivalve.

5

The thin end of the wedge thrusts underneath
The side that's formed a seal with the earth,
A fit as fast and intimate as death.
The lever urges change, release, rebirth.
But the mind, settled in its cozy ditch,
Clothed with the tufted moss of its neurosis,
Which, it believes, will always burn and itch,
Resists, of course, loving its painful stasis.
And change, even extended to the moon,
Even if leaned on by an angel mob
To whom the earth weighs no more than a pin,
Won't budge it, if the mind will not give up.
Before you're tipped from one life to another,
You have to want this miracle to occur.

6

Outside my door I keep an angel chained.
I never feed him, never let him loose,
And no one has accused me of abuse,
Although I wouldn't care if they complained.
I like the way he looks as if he strained
To put his two carved wooden wings to use
And still stood still, impassive and abstruse,
Aware of all he *could* do and disdained.

And that is our relationship. He stands,
For now, where I have put him. His restraint
Is no more and no less than what it seems.
An angel doesn't have to be a saint.
They fall like us, then try to make amends,
As when he comes and pleads with me in dreams.

7

"God is in the details."

Albert Einstein

In which of these details does God inhere?
The woman's head in the boy's lap? His punctured lung?
The place where she had bitten through her tongue?
The drunk's truck in three pieces? The drunk's beer,
Tossed from the cooler, made to disappear?
The silk tree whose pink flowers overhung
The roadside and dropped limp strings among
The wreckage? The steering column, like a spear?

Where in the details, the cleverness of man
To add a gracenote God might understand,
Does God inhere, cold sober, thunderstruck?
I think it's here, in this one: the open can
The drunk placed by the dead woman's hand,
Telling her son, who cried for help, "Good luck."

8

He loads his weapons, but the Lord God sees him.
He hears the inner voice that tells him, "Yes,"
The voice that tells him, "No." And the Lord sees him,
Watching as he listens first to one voice,
A melody, then the other, like a latch
That slips and catches, slips, until it clicks.
The Lord God sees the hard decision taken,
Watching with his seven compound eyes,
As intimate as starlight, as detached.
He sees between the victims and the killer
Each angle of trajectory. Unshaken,
He sees the horror dreamed and brought to being
And still maintains his vigil and his power,
Which you and I would squander with a scream.

9

Someone is always praying as the plane
Breaks up, and smoke and cold and darkness blow
Into the cabin. Praying as it happens,
Praying before it happens that it won't.
Someone was praying that it never happen
Before the first window on Kristallnacht
Broke like a wine glass wrapped in bridal linen.
Before it was imagined, someone was praying
That it be unimaginable. And then,
The bolts blew off and people fell like bombs
Out of their names, out of the living sky.
Surely, someone was praying. And the prayer
Struck the blank face of earth, the ocean's face,
The rockhard, rippled face of facelessness.

10

Have healed the flesh and changed the mind of weather,
Have girdled blacked-out towers with lightning flashes,
Have turned the rose when it began to wither,
Have drawn to inside straights and royal flushes—
With prayer, that gesture out into the blankness,
Beyondness, nothingness, the shaftless mine
That faith worms through, extracting in its thankless
Miracle-making task for lucky men
And women answers to their every prayer.
Have not, however, ended poverty
Or hatred (we will always hate the poor)
Or made the heart into a laboratory
To love the world away from making war
Or taken to what was what things always were.

11

This boy listening eagerly to his friend
Who wears a steel-studded leather wristband
And catechizes him in petty theft
(The kind that leaves a shop clerk dead for pennies)—
This boy, if you could grab him by the wrist
And contradict his thug worship with visions,
As real as TV, of his life in prison,
Might transfer his attention unto you.
But what about his friend? Too late for him?
Before he enters the quick stop and reveals
The weapon he will use to beat or kill
The man or woman breathing behind the counter,
He pulls a nylon stocking over his head.
Look for the sacred face inside that face.

God does not know, God is what is known.
For affirmation ask the living bone.
God does not love, God is what is loved.
Ask flesh in which the skeleton is gloved.
God does not judge, God is what is judged.
Ask rock, ask mountains that the ice has budged.
God is not obeyed, God obeys
And lines up when we stop to count our days.
God is not life, God is what is lived.
And our lives must be seen to be believed.
God is not death, God is what survives.
On certain days all creatures love their lives.
God is not creation, God creates.
Consider things made by our loves and hates.

II

13

Blessèdness—not only in a face
But in the air surrounding everybody,
The charged air that makes me see a body
As blessed just because it has a face.
To feel like that, thoroughly and wholly,
Because someone has just become herself,
Because in seeing I've become myself,
A halved reality completed, wholly.
And then to look at everyone this way,
Like a messenger sending forth a ray
Of gilded light that everywhere announces
That everything is pregnant with itself.
"Rejoice!" I want to say. "You are yourself."
And the mask of meanness turns aside and winces.

All she remembers from her Latin class
Is a phrase she echoes for her granddaughter.
Lately I hear in everything she says
A depth that she covers up with laughter.
In the road is a well. But in her mind
It fills with blanks, like a shaft of sand and pebbles.
A well is in the road. It is profound,
I'm sure, it is a phrase with many levels.
And then, I see one: the woman with five husbands
Met Jesus there. But my mother had only one—
Unless now having lost him she understands
That he was never who she thought, but someone
Who was different men with different women through
         the years.
In the road is a well. It fills with tears.

15

She is a cloud in her own sunny day,
The damp spot on a rock under the lip.
She is the flaw that cracks the fired clay,
The bubble that will break the binding slip.
She is the world after the rapture comes,
The one left in the field, the one left grinding.
History over, she's the drop that drums
In drainpipes without anybody minding.
She is the definition of alone.
And I am one who makes things up about her,
The way the sky makes weather for the earth.
And she is one who lets that happen to her,
The way the dirt will let you take a stone
Into your hand and calculate its worth.

16

And if when he returned he found his mother
Behind the stone that rolled away for him,
Her muscles limp, her memory grown dim,
Unable to respond when he said, "Mother?"
And if he even recognized his mother,
Her outer light and inner light both dim,
Would he do for her what had been done for him?
Would God's son give a new life to his mother?

I think he would balk. And I know why.
And I know this will sound unorthodox,
For she, like any mother, would have given
A kidney if she could have or an eye
To see her boy alive. The paradox
Is that he'd rather see her safe in heaven.

A living room. Gray walls and carpet, light.
Gray window curtains pulled both day and night.
Gray couch and gray, stuffed chairs lapping the floor
With stiff upholstery skirts. The glum decor,
As memory employs its narrow lens,
A shadowing of picture edges, bookends,
And in a central place the TV set,
Its blank face gray or green, a sleeping pet.
No action.   Yet the eyes are focused on
A sudden apparition in a chair
Who flares up like the vision of a god
And blinds them, and intones, "This is my son,
In whom I am not pleased." Then, the eyes clear,
And someone else sees with them after that.

Everything around the central meaning,
Whatever grips that something in the womb
And, when a door slams, looks as if it's leaning
From all the objects in a startled room;
Everything that passes through the puzzle
A spider glues together or is caught,
And bends the whisker back until the muzzle
Twitches, and tugs, then loosens the square knot;
Everything surrounding everything
That's going to happen, even the manger's planks,
The barn's stone lintels, poised as if to sing,
The angel choir of matter giving thanks;
And all that made the world seem passing strange:
Everything is about to know a change.

Everything is about to know a change,
For someone will appear and say a word,
And someone else will hear and rearrange
His life as no one ever thought he would.
And something like an earthquake or a storm
Will happen somewhere like a little town,
And that place, although nothing but a stem,
Will snap off and the tree will tumble down.
And the about-to-be, a secret cache,
Will smoulder like a spark inside a couch,
And those who sat in darkness, dropping ash,
Will see a great light. Everyone will touch

And be touched by the change no one can stop.
A single leaf will speak. A voice will drop.

A voice will speak. A single leaf will drop.
And the whole tree will wither where it stands
And never bear again, though he could help,
As he has helped the withered bones of hands,
The corneas of clouded over eyes,
The blood and breath of loved ones, dead and dying,
And even water, calming frantic seas,
And even water, turning it to wine.
The poor world must have fallen with the fall
For him to curse a fruit tree, out of season,
For giving nothing, like an unborn apple,
And then to make up, for some obscure reason,
A lesson on the power of faith and prayer.
Perhaps to understand, you had to be there.

Perhaps to understand you had to be
Alone with the absent presence he called father,
Alone with the dysfunctional family
Of stars and darkness, deaf and dumb together,
And in that interaction see a sign,
The way a bedside watcher will believe
A twitch or flicker—almost anything—
Is proof the injured sleeper will revive.
Perhaps to understand, you had to die,
Having acknowledged with your body's pain
That everybody does, unmythically,

Knowing only that it won't happen again,
And then to wake and find your death the proof
Of an abstraction that the world calls love.

The abstraction that the world calls love
Appeared to grieving friends and cooked them food
And walked with them a way and let one shove
Fingers into his wounds and take a good
Look. And then he turned to wind and fire
And pieces of his clothes and eyelashes
And thorns and rusty nails and locks of hair
And red letters on a few translucent pages.
He took on flesh and then he took it off,
Or else he kept it for a souvenir,
Or else—but why keep going back and forth?
He dwelt among us, then he disappeared.
And we are left to be and keep on being,
Like everything around a central meaning.

19

The devil comes on the air waves, crooning
Soft Christian rock songs in a cartoon voice,
Loops of self-love and pity wound through swooning
Melodies stamped from saccharine and noise.
And then he says that they are songs I wrote—
And pulls in choruses of friends and teachers
And enemies and people on the street,
To sing along, against their better natures.
But where's the speaker? Where's the radio?
Some filling in my head that's come alive?
It's in my head all right, with video
That flickers all day and focuses at night.
I'll have to find a way to turn it off
Or change the channel, let alone my life.

20

One model asks another, "What do you eat?"
She means how do you keep your skeleton
Just underneath your skin, how do you con
Your soul as if it were an appetite?
The kingdom is within you, Tolstoy said.
My grandfather could put his finger on
The spot he felt the flame of spirit burn,
And it was not some vague thing in his head.
Tolstoy looked straight at nakedness bedecked
With all the jewels of empire and still saw
What lay beyond desire, cooked or raw,
And wanted heaven more than intellect.
You, too, can stay as thin as Jesus Christ,
Eating down to the perfume of your wrist.

Think of the harsh attire that God put on,
Improved with vitamins and vaccinations,
Anointed, toned, massaged with gleaming lotions,
Heart-smart and fiber-dieted and trim:
A body more like ours, aerobic, clean,
Groomed properly, with proper dental care,
Modern and made to last, at least in theory,
More than a stingy three score years and ten.
Now there's a corpse to translate into heaven.
The truth is no one wants to leave the world,
Unless nothing has worked and all has broken
Down into pain. Then, even God would suffer
Less with carbon monoxide in a can,
Breathed in the comfort of a private van.

What will we give up in the after life,
When we have been enhanced to a higher power
And all the goodness of the body made so pure
Its quantum leap will have to feel like loss?
In our spirit flesh, *pneumatikon*
(Though the Greek sounds like a mattress): to see
Will be to take; to wish for, have; to sigh
Will be the sign of utter satisfaction.
But what about that instant of desire
Before we're gratified, the rapturous waiting
On this side of epiphany and climax?
Without the lapse of time, we'll lose that pleasure,
The unique arousal of previsioning,
The thrill in scenting that first cup of coffee.

23

How long was their grief—so inconsolable—
With a friend's place empty at the table?
Not long at all. In less than a weekend
All the deadened senses were reawakened
And the blurred world focused to a new vision.
Anyone stricken with real deprivation
Hasn't hit the bottom in three days.
They were spared years of weeping, numbness, haze.
Everything, really. Ask the truly bereft,
The losers of all hope, the loved and left,
Who know the weight of ashes and cold clay.
These were bumping into the dead one not long after
And breaking bread with him in tears and laughter.
They were celebrating by the third day.

24

Breath like a house fly batters the shut mouth.
The dream begins, turns over, and goes flat.
The virus cleans the attic and heads south.
Somebody asks, "What did you mean by that?"
But nobody says, "Nothing," in response.
Silence becomes the question and the answer.
The ghost abandons all of his old haunts.
The body turns a last cell into cancer.
And then—banal epiphany—and then,
Time kick starts and the deaf brain hears a voice.
The eyes like orphans find the world again.
Day washes down the city streets with noise.
And oxygen repaints the blood bright red.
How good it is to come back from the dead!

III

25

Nothing but pleasure in the bottle's voice
As the cork pulls from its neck. Nothing, as
The wine finds its legs in the bell of the glass,
But pleasure, on the lips, on the tongue, in the muscles
And veins of the throat. And though darkness hovers above
The candle flames, there is only pleasure when
The face flushes and the lover sees it. Only
Pleasure somehow in that redness and that witness,
As the food (some dish prepared for the pure pleasure of it)
Is consumed. Pleasure, a small god, absent
From the vast and crowded morgues of heaven and hell,
Is our true god. As the lovers disrobe and embrace
And nakedness becomes as delectable
As butter and olive oil, only pleasure watches.

Ray's body lies below a slab that states
His surname, *Jarman*. Ray, in his coffin, wears
A colored hood and robe with black felt bars.
Ray's flesh is safe from worms and graveyard rats.
On that day when his soul (which in heaven sits
Surrounded by the answers to his prayers)
Rejoins his body to be judged, he fears
(And these fears plague his secret, heavenly thoughts)
That he will have to be the age forever
That he was when he died, that he will be
The way he was, attempting to recover,
At eighty-three, in his clerical array,
From stroke-slurred speech, his halting, stunned
       endeavor
To end the thing that he'd begun to say.

27

We crowded in the taxi. It was dawn
And just as cold inside as where we'd stood
Apart, as strangers. Cramped, I felt we could
Touch and draw warmth, and still remain withdrawn.
But when I settled down and tried to yawn,
The others broke the silence, talking food
And which internal organs they found good
In flesh and fowl. We hit the autobahn
And one said she thought hearts were hard to chew.
As soft as caramel, another said,
If you'll just let them simmer in a stew.
That's when an idea froze inside my head,
While they yakked on, the giblet-loving crew,
And I knew this was hell and I was dead.

I'll bet the final reckoning's like this:
That brilliant day in Swansea, in the park
Across the street from Thomas's birthplace,
My camera pointed everywhere to mark
In light the record of our happiness,
My daughters on the swings, his poetry
Among the garden stones, the Bristol Channel—
The North Atlantic's Welsh and English kennel—
Beyond the Mumbles Lighthouse. You could see
All the way to heaven's old address.
I thought I caught it all, a floating spark
Of memory that film would surely fix,
Only to learn the cog-slipped roll was dark
And blank as Lethe and the River Styx.

29

"Here is the soul." He pointed to a place
That in the dream was right between his eyes.
On waking I could not recall his face
Or how I knew the soul was just the size
Of sunset tangled in a hill of trees.
The soul, a cloud of blood inside his skull,
Poured out between his eyes onto his knees
And coiled like snakeskin or a skein of wool.
"Here is the soul," he said again. But I
Knew better now—inside the now of dreaming.
I knew that if I looked him in the eye
And said, "That is the soul," the truth of seeming
Would overwrite the truth of being, kill it,
And if there was a wound, my soul would fill it.

Kenosis

An absence turned to presence is confusing.
Take Mary, who took for a gardener
One that she knew was dead and in his grave,
One that she then called Master, when he stood
Before her and said, "Mary," and resisted
Her startled, tender, human wish to touch.
We want to fill the emptiness with meaning.
I had a friend whose father died in his armchair.
And when my friend came home, there was a drape
With the body slumped beneath it, still in the chair.
She said, "I knew that must be him. And yet,
It was a shock to see him sitting there,
So present and not present, this big man,
Filling his place as much or more than ever."

Emmaus

They're eating dinner with someone they loved,
Someone almost forgotten from their past,
Who has come back. And they are all amazed
And look on as they chew, as their friend talks
And breaks a fresh loaf open, and remarks

It's *like* something, and offers it to them
And says it yields up truth like a sweet savor.
They put their noses to the fractured crust.
But it's not bread they're breathing. It is words.
And then, they are alone, thinking of things
To ask that now they can't. What's a "sweet savor"?
And all they have is right before their eyes,
Bread crumbs, some honey, and a piece of fish,
All of which tastes like joy and disbelief.

Damascus

Headlong in your career, breathing out threatenings
And slaughter against enemies, dictating trouble
For anyone advanced ahead of you, gambling
That you can stay ahead of your rep, checking off
The list of those to chop off at the top, and the place
Your name will be inked in, all the while businesslike,
Congenial with associates and flattering
To authorities and enforcers, bloody and obscene
Only in private mutterings and unspoken dreams,
On your way to yet another hanging, stoning, gossip-
Mongering swap meet of assassins, you're surprised
As much as anyone to be chosen—though it requires
A certain blindness on your part and such a change
You wouldn't know yourself—a vessel of grace.

Patmos

On a clear day you can see dark matter—
And still not know what you are looking at.
Or turn and see the simple heavens shatter
And make themselves into an alphabet
Of riddles wrapped inside of mysteries
Inside enigmas, coming from deep space.
What do you do when everything's a sign
And the goatskin of the universe uncaps
And pours its missing mass out like a wine?
I saw the script that glares inside rubbed eyes.
I felt the infrastructure of the face
That will endure though empires collapse.
I was astonished, I could hardly speak,
And wrote it all down afterwards, in Greek.

31

Put on the costume jewelry and chapeau,
Turn to the camera, to the winking god's-eye
Whose gaze you tolerate, whose gleam you know
As light recording you, your look, your body.

Step into the embrace of what you love,
The wonderfully smooth coherence of live touch,
Somebody's aching voice, the held note of
Your name, the only thing that matters much.

If nothing's in the temple, then the eyes
Will worship what is there: the body first
Or body image first, the numinous
Replacement for the soul, the *I* as *it*.
And why not try the concept on for size?
If nothing is sacred, we can worship it.

There is a law outside the daily racket,
The vertigo of distracting personal woes,
And one outside of that, and beyond those,
The one that fits the cosmos like a jacket.
And when I think of that—that big abstraction—
I feel like a retiree in Palm Springs.
The serene, tearless clarity of things
Settles me down into sublime inaction.

But I am not a retiree in Palm Springs.
The girls of anxious gravity, my sin,
Tug at my heart and pockets, and I spin,
Bracing myself against a storm of things
That pelt and paw me and caress and claw—
The law inside the law inside the law.

Lord, spare me from the drowsiness that starts
Just as I put my finger on a word.
Erase the errands I think to do instead.
Don't let me leave my desk. Don't let me parse
The day into voluptuous repetitions,
The three square meals, the necessary chores,
The naps extending eros into boredom
(Those sexy daydreams I do nothing with).
Lord, stop my hand when it begins to sketch
The intricate, useless doodle in the margin,
And bring it to my mouth to close the yawn
That ends the day before it even begins.
Make me equal to the task, and make the task
The goading preoccupation of a lifework.

34

Although I know God's immanence can speak
In sunlight's parallels and intersections;
Although I know the spiritual technique
For finding God in all things, when I pray
It is to nothing manifest at all.
And though I know it's merely technical,
I do not pray to nothing. Yesterday,
One of those offhand, razor-edged rejections
The world flips like a Frisbee grazed my cheek.
It drew blood. No consoling recollections
Of having shaken off that sort of play
Helped me forget it. I could not recall
My strength, and brooded, lost and tragical,
Till, marking this blank page, I found a way.

The yellow blister wears a ring of red.
King Christ will pick among the quick and dead.
The black nail hangs, half-hinged, a beetle's wing.
The Lord is not a person, place, or thing.
Ignore the canker sore another day.
The Virgin stares at candles in a tray.
Hair sheds on the fat pillow during sleep.
High heaven is as vague as hell is deep.
Deep in an obscure chamber of the ear
A phone rings. No one answers. For a year.
And then another year. And then there comes
The Saint of Getting-Used-To-It, with drums
To drown the irritation in white noise,
Until the final silence and its cause.

He will not let us blame Him easily.
When steel enforcement cracks the concrete slab
And rain finds all the victims breezily,
And stained debris is taken to the lab,
He will not let us curse His name and die.
Our tasks define the days ahead like hopes.
A flask contains His airtight alibi.
The rubble's wrapped in existential tropes.
Why should He get the credit but no blame?
All of one good day the weather held
And the floors held, as we worked from above.
And bodies each began to find a name.
It didn't matter how many had been killed.
He'd tell us that the aftermath is love.

IV

I can't do more than this. I can't do less—
To choose a target adamant as death
And try to find a way to make it bend.
Try faith and insult. Even try to bless
Annihilation for its selflessness.
Try cool indifference. Try a lust for life.
Blue smoke by day and mirror-fire by night.
Try forcing imagination to confess,
In the strict silence of the infinite spaces,
That it was made for filling in the blanks,
For drawing features on the empty faces,
Including death's, and reading them like books.
Try reading, then, the writing on the face
That blunts immortal and industrial diamonds.

38

I need an image for the soul and choose
The selfish gene that wants to live forever,
Maker of heaven, the spike inside the fever,
The unit that can't help but reproduce.
It looks back at me from the sexless face
Of sex and shows its triumph over death,
Emerging from beneath the bridal lace
Imagination spreads to hide the earth.
The brain that holds the sky, the blood of stars,
The breathing skin with all its sacred doors,
All have been manufactured to ensure
That one inhuman engine will endure.
I need an image for the soul, and would
Choose something else entirely if I could.

39

Which ones should I believe among the voices
Chanting my name as though it were a spell
To save a life or send one straight to hell?
Which ones are singing, which ones merely noises,
The backfiring of cherubs in Rolls Royces?
And which belong to those who kiss and tell
Me my own secrets? Which crow or philomel
Croaks sadly when I fail and which rejoices?

I tell myself that I should listen only
To the good, that receding caller-after
Of blessings, like a mother at the door;
And not, when scoured inside out and lonely,
To that one that produces distant laughter
And makes me wonder what it's laughing for.

40

History happening and people living
While you are not. And as for your non-presence,
Nobody knows of it or needs you yet.
People alive in life and history happening.
And where you will be one day: plenty of space
And time, like fractions deep inside of π,
The genes of its irrationality,
Just waiting for division to locate them.
Wherever you fit, elbowing your survival
Into its niche of habit and surprise,
A handful of machines that share your codes,
And would spill blood to save them, will surround you.
Meanwhile, between the egg and sperm—oblivion,
Gossip of sweet delight and endless night.

Fallen persimmons among the dew-bent grasses,
Poking their heads up like emerging planets,
Orange as sunrise, soften, split, and wrinkle.
Stepped on, they turn to paste. Still, they delight
The wasps and butterflies that come in daylight
And the opossum in the predawn hours
Who, when the headlights catch her feeding, scuttles
On pink feet down the driveway to the shadows.
They drop through the damp night like phases of dreaming,
A muchness Keats would marry to an ode,
With tannin on the skin like memory,
Delicious to all tongues. Yes, that's the life—
To make your peace in sleep and half asleep
And change the world around you once a year.

42

Instead, you can walk backwards into life—
Undo your steps and gain ground as you yield,
As long as ground remains beneath your feet.
It's like one way of wading into surf,
Putting the swell behind you as it breaks.
The other is to take life diving under
With eyes shut tight until it washes over.
Either way, if you don't want to face
The world mounting towards you, wave on wave,
Or setting up its obstacles perversely,
You can make a virtue of reversal
Or submission. Then, perhaps, you'll have
That certain feeling of being vaguely shepherded
Or that someone somewhere knows where you are headed.

43

So many creatures and so many minds.
Such thicknesses of skin and consciousness.
So many gross and delicate designs
That pierce the lantern of the human face.
So many faces. And such deep desire
To break into another person's soul
And loot it or just look to see what's there—
A country or a room, a hill or hole.

The greatest rupture, William James has said,
In all creation is from mind to mind.
As if to keep your thinking to yourself
Were not a gift, to wish another dead
And yet in passing ask after his health
Were not a way of loving our own kind.

The gift for all our waking in this life,
For every time a bad night spoiled the day
With back pain or a sour frame of mind;
The sure reward for staying wide awake
Through buzzing monologues of hours and minutes,
The self-obsession of our span of years;
The grace that is a distant field of vision,
Not like exhaust haze warped by traffic heat,
But spindrift rising from the edge of earth;
The prize for suffering our names, for knowing
More than we thought we knew and knowing less;
The promise of an end like our beginning,
Oblivious to boredom, pain, and hope,
Is, said the man, a dreamless, mindless sleep.

He passes through the rolled-up warehouse door,
Onto the dock, a plate of tempered glass,
The poet whose work was also tough and clear.
The daylight reads him with a blunt caress.
His destination is a shopfront window square,
Facing an empty street in a failed downtown
They're trying to bring back. He will watch there,
Gazing beyond as, once, he gazed within.
Now men with gloved hands stow him on a truck.
The gears engage, the engine's violence
Trembles in the silence of his look.
The world glides like a thought across his face.
And he stares through it, like a library
Of emptiness and fullness, like a sky.

Larry Levis, 1946-1996

The moon is such a good thing to come back to,
Like the good dream in which a long lost friend
Returns from death and is once more your friend
And, though you have forgotten him, forgives you.
Of course, among the stars and before dawn,
The reason that the moon seems so alive,
When it is truly, deeply not alive,
Is moonlight, and the face that it puts on.

The moon sets at the dead end of our street,
Above a house where someone wrote a song,
Above graves where some people have been buried
Over a hundred years. Right down the street,
It shines like it belongs in an old song
That might wake people who have long been buried.

47

I laid it out, how A would beat its wings
And set off tidal forces against B,
Which with a spasm would repel toward C
The waves that D would organize in rings,
Letting them spread, until I tugged the strings
That pulled them all together perfectly.
And everything would end up beautifully.
That would be that. And that would settle things.

And then my friend, a kindly Rabelaisian,
Aware that I thought this was in the can,
Took a drag, a drink, shook earth with a cough,
And asked if I knew how to make God laugh.
Dazed by my brilliance, I didn't get the question.
He paused for breath, then whispered, "Have a plan."

The world works for us and we call it grace.
It works against us and, if we are brave,
We call it nothing and we keep our faith,
And only to ourselves we call it fate.
What makes the world work? No one seems to know.
The clouds arrange the weather, the sea goes
Deep, a black stillness seethes at the earth's core,
And somebody invents the telephone.
If we are smart, we know where we fit in.
If we are lucky, we know what to bid.
If we are good, we know a charming fib
Can do more good than harm. So we tell it.
The world was meant to operate like this.
The working of the world was ever thus.

The working of the world was ever thus.
The empty air surrounds us with its love.
A fire in the skull ignites the sun.
The skin of water opens at a touch.
And earth erupts, earth curves away, earth yields.
Someone imagines strife and someone peace.
Someone inserts the god in the machine
And someone picks him out like a poppy seed.
In every new construction of desire,
The old dissatisfactions rule the eyes.
The new moon eats the old and, slice by slice,
Rebuilds a face of luminous delight,

In which we see ourselves, at last, make sense.
It is the mirror in everything that shines.

It is the mirror in everything that shines
And makes the soul the color of the sky
And clarifies and gradually blinds
And shows the spider its enormous bride.
And we show our reluctant gratitude,
Searching the paths and runways for a spoor
Of cosmic personality, one clue,
Even the fossil light of burned-out proof.
It is enough and not enough to sketch
The human mask inside the swarming nest
And hold the face, a template, to the egg
And stamp its features on the blank of death.
Although we break rock open to find life,
We cannot stare the strangeness from the leaf.

We cannot stare the strangeness from the leaf,
And so we spin all difference on a wheel
And blur it into likeness. So we seize
The firefly and teach it human need
And mine its phosphor for cold light and call
Across the world as if it were a lawn,
Blinking awake at summer dusk. We talk
Ceaselessly to things that can't respond
Or won't respond. What are we talking for?
We're talking to coax hope and love from zero.
We're talking so the brain of the geode

Will listen like a garden heliotrope
And open its quartz flowers. We are talking
Because speech is a sun, a kind of making.

Because speech is a sun, a kind of making,
And muteness we have always found estranging,
Because even our silences are phrasing
And language is the tongue we curl for naming,
Because we want the earth to be like heaven
And heaven to be everywhere we're headed,
Because we hope our formulae, like hexes,
Will stop and speed up time at our behesting,
There is no help for us, and that's our glory.
A furious refusal to acknowledge,
Except in words, the smallness of our portion,
Pumps heart, lights brain, and conjures up a soul
From next to nothing. We know all flesh is grass.
And when the world works, we still call it grace.

Today is fresh, and yesterday is stale.
Today is fast, and yesterday is slow.
Today is yes, and yesterday is no.
Today is news, and yesterday's a tale.
The grave is empty. Last night it was full.
The glorious means of death was once a shame.
Someone is God who had a common name
That you might give a child or animal.
It happens overnight. The world is changed.
The bottles in the cellar all decant.
The stars sign the new cosmos at a slant.
And everybody's plans are rearranged.
Today we meet our maker, in a flash
That turns the ash of yesterday to flesh.